We love Walking with Wildlife Colouring Book

This book belongs to _____

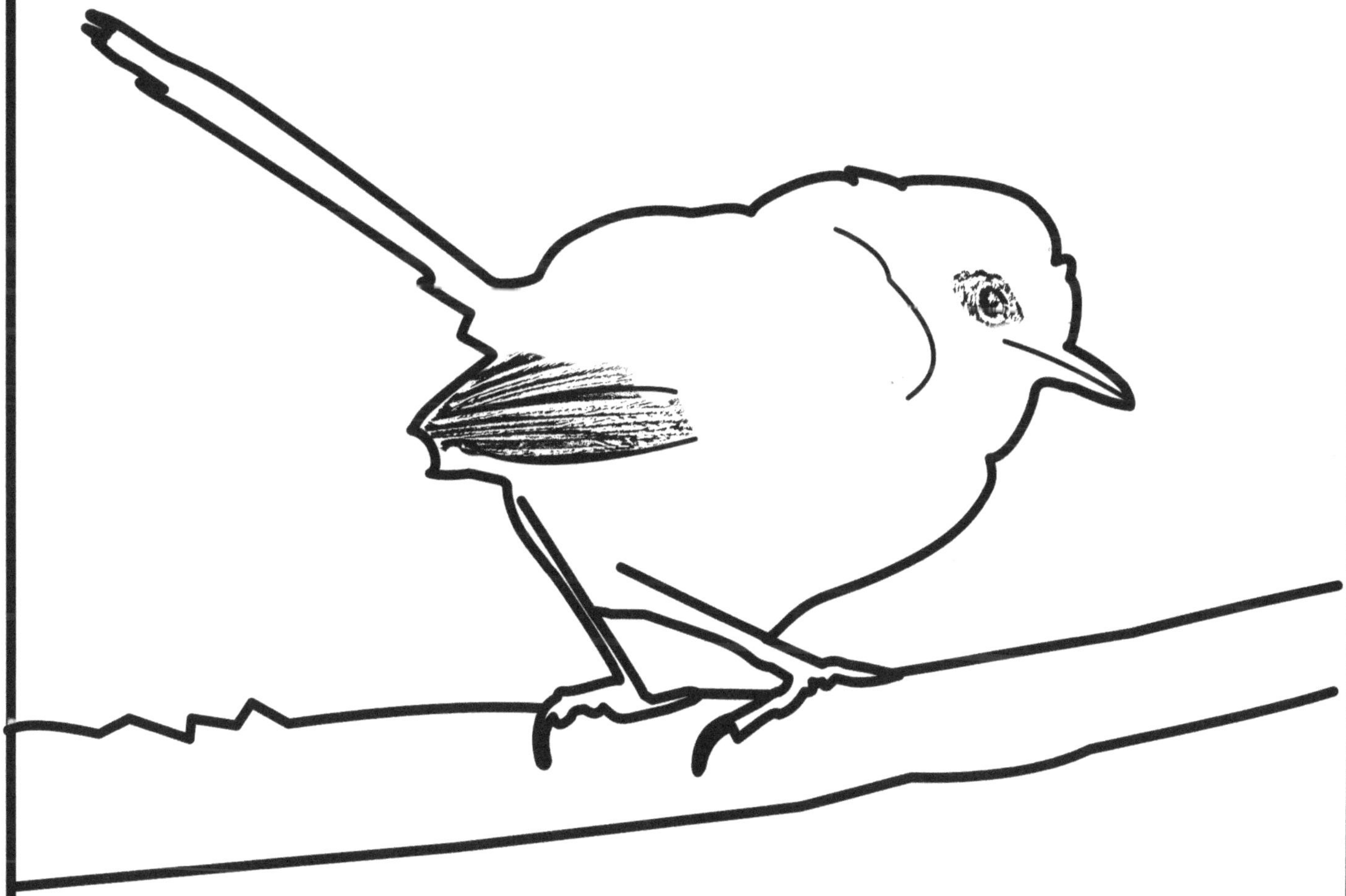

Written and Illustrated
By Jenny Dyer

First Published 2025 by Jenny Dyer

For further information
contact through facebook pages

***Walking with Wildlife*™**
and
JD's Snaps and Designs

Text: © Jennifer Dyer 2025
Photography: © Jennifer Dyer 2025

All rights reserved. No part of this publication may be reproduced, stored in a retrieval system, or transmitted in any form or by any means electronic or mechanical, or by photocopying or otherwise without prior written permission of the author or copyright holder.

ISBN 978-1-7637939-5-8

Cover and Artwork: Jenny Dyer

This colouring book can be used as a stand-alone colouring book or as a companion book to the Walking with Wildlife series as most of the illustrations are based on photos from these books:

Walking With Wildlife - Children's Book about Observing Wildlife (Available in both Hard Cover or Perfect Bound Editions}

Walking With Wildlife - Book 2 - Watching Bird Behaviour (Available in both Hard Cover or Perfect Bound Editions}

Walking With Wildlife - Book 3 - Can You Count The Animals? (Perfect Bound)

Colour Test Page

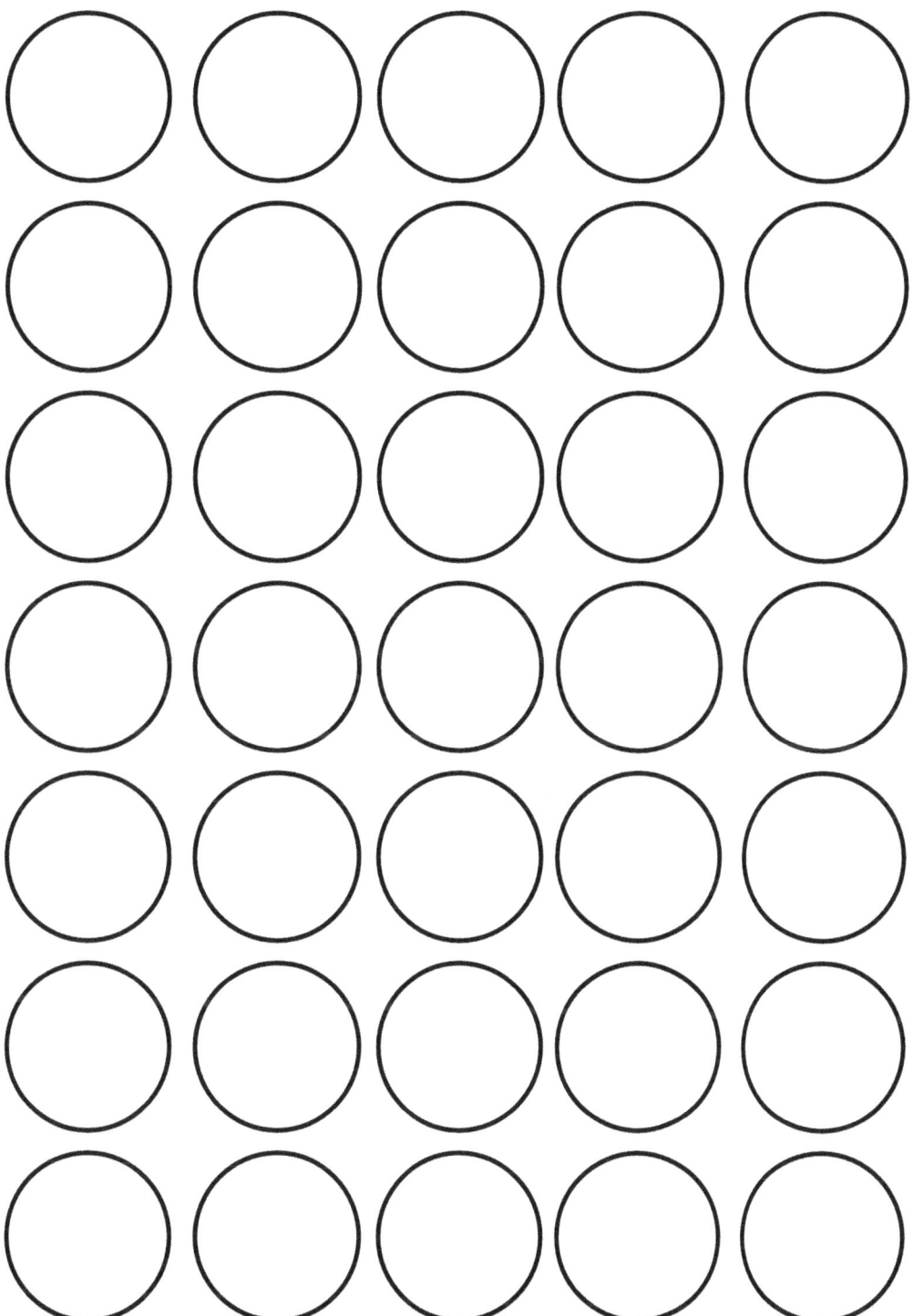

Walking with Wildlife™ © Jenny Dyer

Red-Backed Fairy Wren

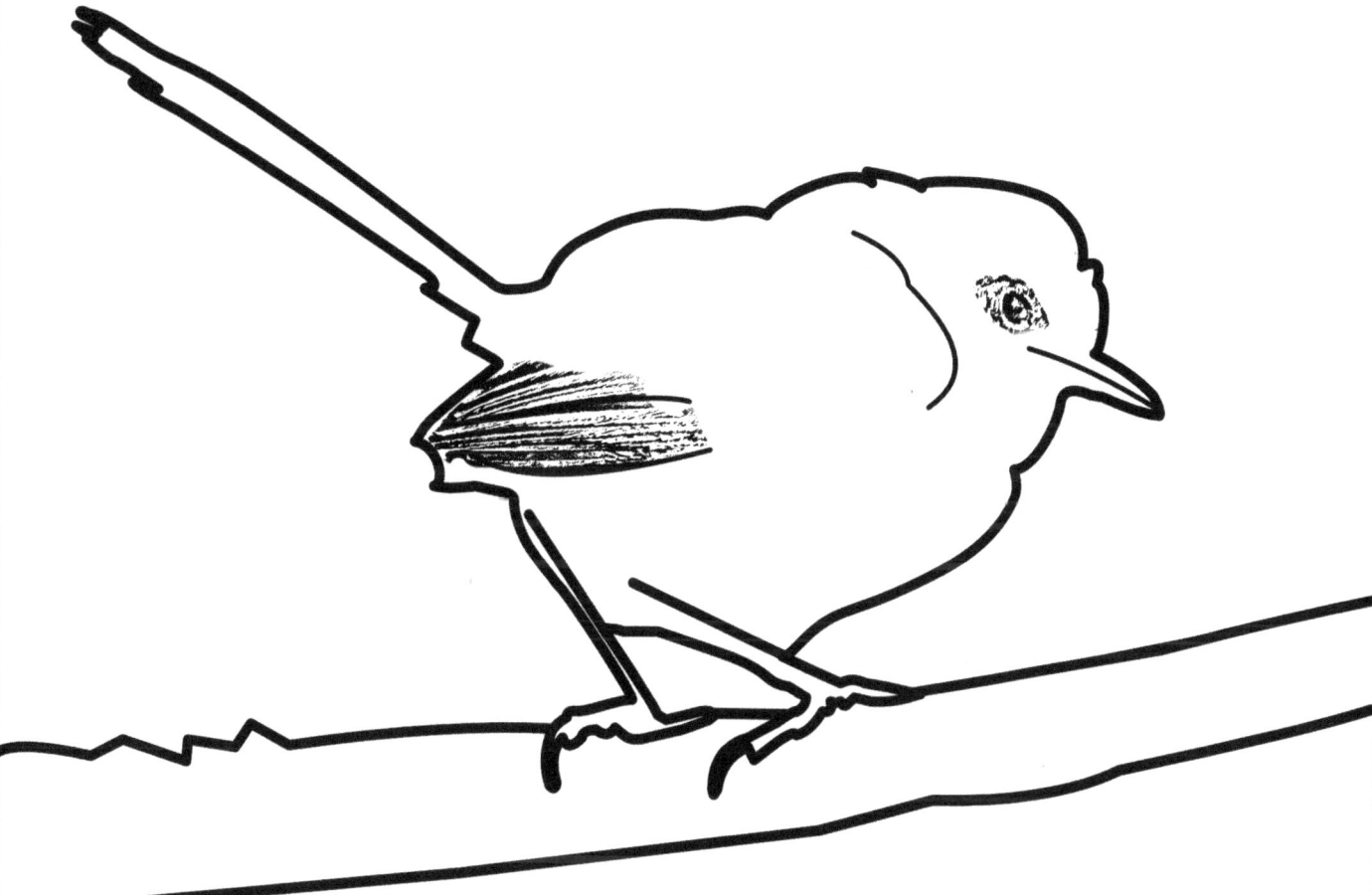

Red-backed fairy wrens live mostly on the grassy flats and will quickly hide in the grass or small shrubs when disturbed. They eat mainly insects but also eat seeds and small fruit. The adult males are black with a red back and the females and young birds are brown. They live in small family groups.

Kangaroo

Kangaroos usually live on the open grass country. They are marsupials which means they carry their young joeys in their pouch where they are fed. All marsupials are mammals which means they feed their young milk.

Blue-Faced Honeyeater

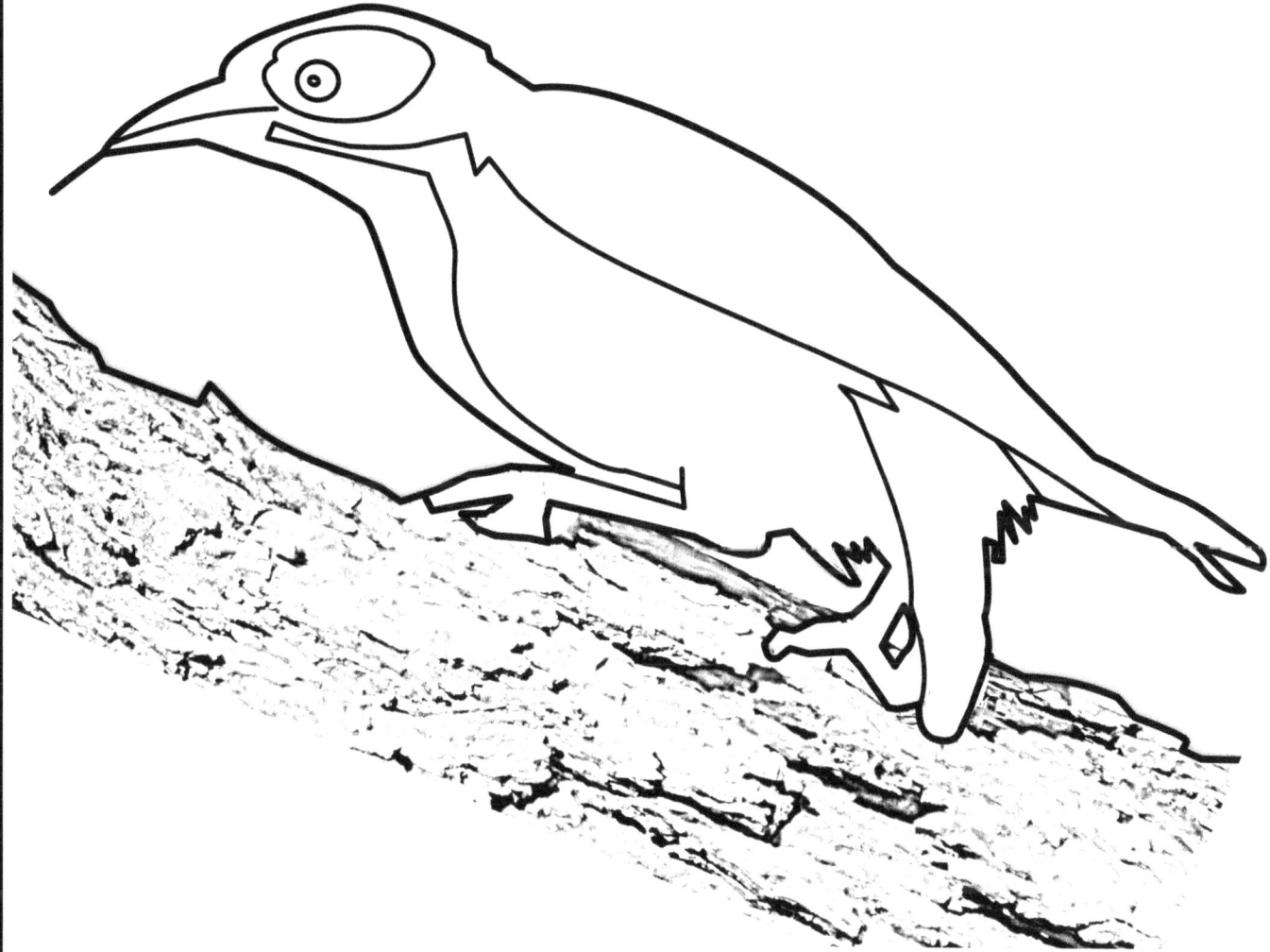

The blue-faced honeyeaters stay in little family groups. They eat fruit, nectar and little insects. Their long sticky tongue helps them catch insects. They can be a pest in orchards and banana plantations as they eat the fruit. The juvenile birds are actually green around the eye but the adults are blue.

Monarch Butterfly

The Monarch Butterfly or Wanderer is not native to Australia but arrived around 1870. The caterpillar of the Monarch Butterfly lives on the wild cotton bushes or milkweed. These winged insects only live for a very short time after they emerge from the chrysalis. They have poison in their bodies that makes predators sick.

Koala

Like the kangaroo, the koala is a marsupial with a pouch to carry its young joey in. They are also nocturnal (awake at night) and they sleep through the day for more than 18 hours. Koalas hide very well in the trees but you can hear them grunting and growling at night. They appear to be very cute, but they have very sharp claws for gripping the branches. Even though some people call them koala bears, they are not actually bears at all.

Chestnut-Breasted Mannikin

The chestnut-breasted mannikin is a finch often seen in large flocks migrating inland in the dry season. They love to feed on grass seeds but will eat winged termites and small insects in the breeding season.

Rainbow Lorikeet

The rainbow lorikeet is a brightly coloured parrot that can hide well in the trees. They like to nest in the hollows of eucalyptus trees and can be aggressive to other birds who come near their nests.

These colourful parrots love native flowers but will also feed on fruit and insects. They can be a pest for the orchard and banana growers.

Willy Wagtail

The willy wagtail chases insects which are his main source of food. They were called willy wagtails because their tails are forever wagging. Willy wagtails are very territorial and will often chase away other bigger birds.

Koala

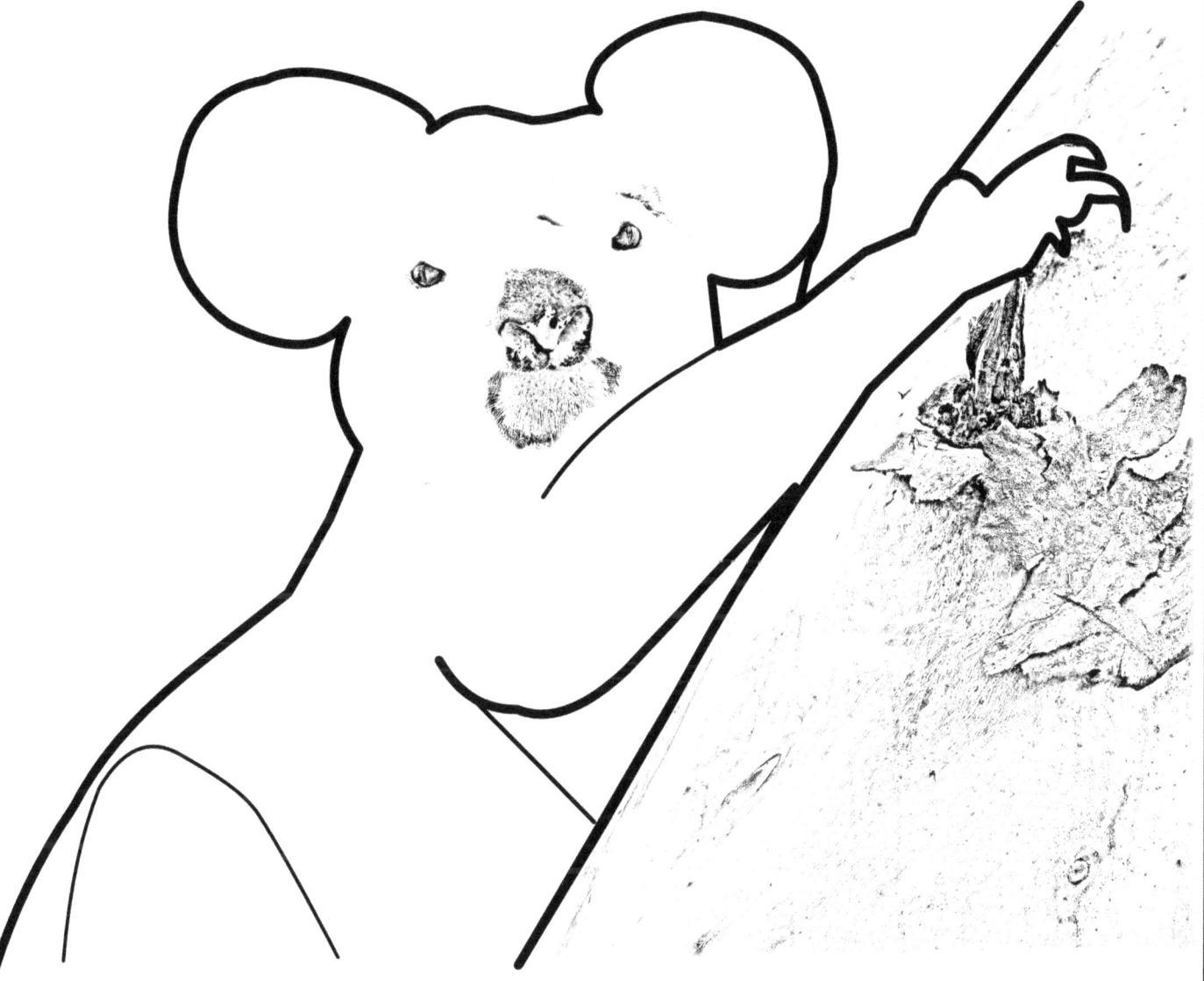

The word 'koala' comes from the aboriginal word for 'no drink' as they don't drink very much water. They get their moisture from the eucalyptus leaves they eat. These leaves are poisonous to most animals but not the koala.

European Bee

The European bee is not usually a danger but will sting if threatened. They are used to produce the honey we love to eat as well as providing wax. They are also used in agriculture to pollinate plants.

Brown Honeyeater

The brown honeyeaters spread pollen and use their tongue to lick. They can hover for short times near flowers but this one preferred to hang upside down.

Brown Honeyeater

The brown honeyeaters spread pollen and use their tongue to lick. They can hover for short times near flowers but this one preferred to hang upside down.

Double-Barred Finch

The double-barred finch is also known as the owl-faced finch. They live in the open grass country and like to eat grass seed. They live in big flocks and often go to drink water together.

Spangled Drongo

The spangled drongo feeds on insects. They are smart birds and will often wait for other birds to find the insects and then swoop in and steal their meal off them. Drongos also eat small birds and lizards.

They will mimic the sound of other animals.

Black-Faced Cuckooshrike

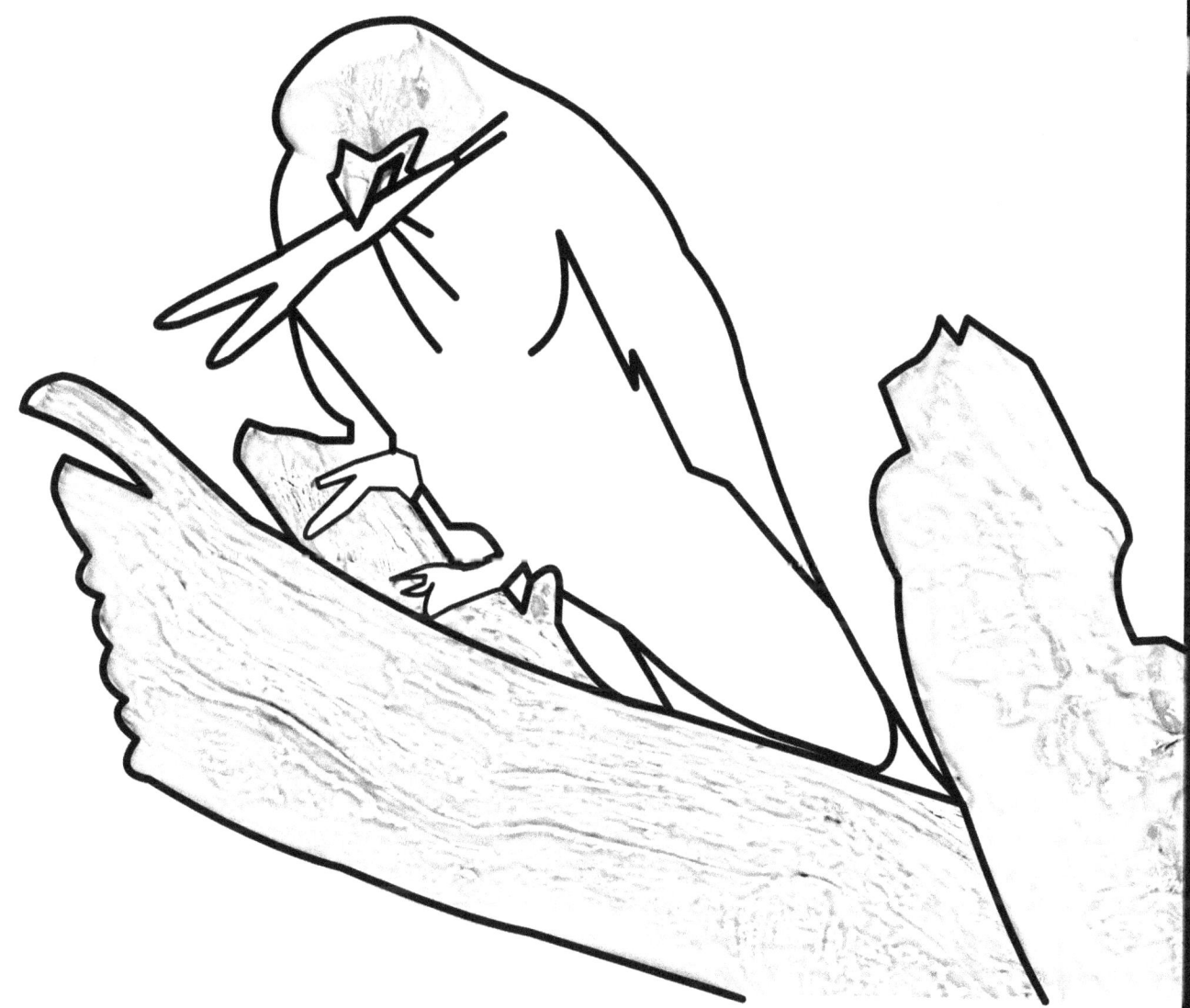

The black-faced cuckooshrike is an omnivore, and eats meat and vegetables. They enjoy insects and their larvae, caterpillars, as well as other invertebrates (earthworms, millipedes, snails, spiders). Sometimes they will eat some fruits and seeds.

Crested Pigeon

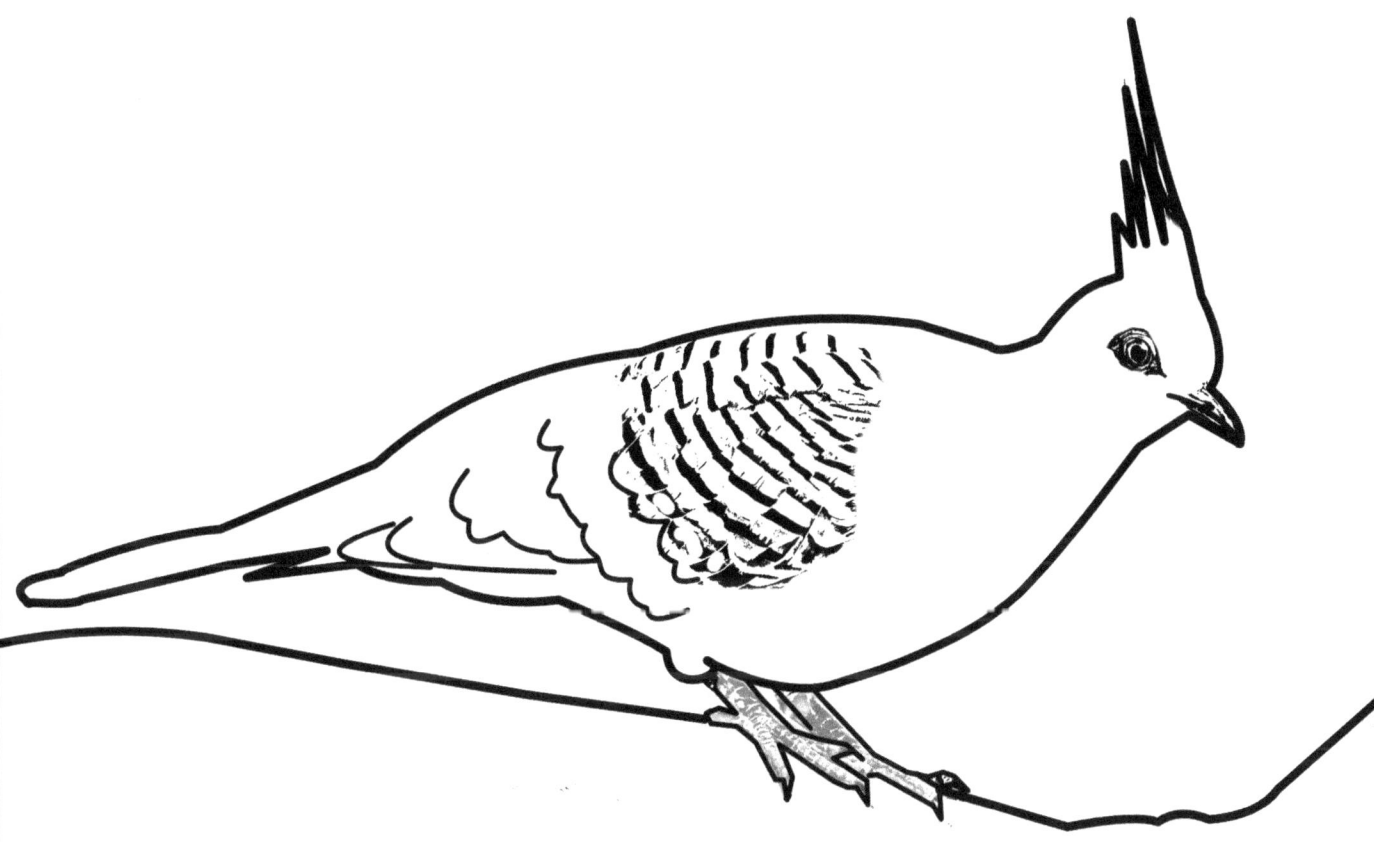

The crested pigeon has very pretty wings which flash iridescent green, bronze and crimson/purple in the sunlight. Their diet includes mostly seeds and leaves but they do eat a small amount of insects and invertebrates.

Grey Butcherbird

The grey butcherbird will hang its prey on barbed wire fences or spiky branches. They eat mainly insects but also small vertebrates (animals that have a backbone or spine) and a little fruit, seeds and nectar.

These feathered friends have the most beautiful song and you can often hear them in the morning.

Grey-Crowned Babbler

Grey-crowned babblers feed mainly in groups on insects and other invertebrates and sometimes eat seeds. You can spot them bouncing along the ground from one insect to the next. Babblers live in small families and you can hear them chattering to each other.

Kookaburra

The laughing kookaburra has a very loud, raucous laugh which signals to other birds that this is his territory. He eats other small animals and can often be seen sitting on a branch or perch ready to swoop down to the ground to catch his prey.

The kookaburra is the largest member of the Kingfisher family.

Noisy Miner

The noisy miner can be aggressive to other birds and try to take over their territory. Noisy miners feed in large family groups on nectar, fruit and insects.

Rainbow Bee-eater

The rainbow bee-eaters tunnel into the ground to make their nests. They eat mainly bees and wasps, as well as dragonflies, beetles, butterflies and moths. This native Australian bird catches the insects in the air then returns to its perch to beat them on the perch before eating them.

Rainbow bee-eaters don't drink much water as they get all the moisture they need from the insects they eat.

Sulphur-Crested Cockatoo

The sulphur-crested cockatoo is a very intelligent bird and has been taught to talk (sometimes not the words you would like to hear). They are very noisy birds and can be heard from a long distance away. These large, white birds eat grass seeds, plants, nuts (especially bunya nuts) and insects.

Plumed Whistling Ducks

The plumed whistling ducks feed on grass seed. They are very stylish ducks with lovely plumage (feathers). They lay ten to twelve eggs in a nest made of grass, hidden in tall grass. The eggs will take up to 30 days to hatch. Both the male and female share sitting on the eggs and looking after the young when they hatch.

Kangaroos

Kangaroos are the largest marsupial on earth and are the only large animals that move by hopping. They have very long, hind feet and a long, strong tail to help them hop.

The kangaroo features on the Australian dollar coin.

A kangaroo is also on our coat of arms alongside the emu because they are found in every Australian state and neither can move backwards easily, symbolizing a country always moving forward.

White-Faced Heron

White-faced herons have long necks that are useful for striking quickly at their prey. You will find them near shallow fresh water where they catch and eat small fish and amphibians (cold-blooded vertebrates that live in water and on land) such as frogs and lizards. You will also see them walking through the grass eating insects.

www.ingramcontent.com/pod-product-compliance
Lightning Source LLC
Chambersburg PA
CBHW040226040426
42333CB00054B/3456